BEST SHOTS

THE GREATEST NFL PHOTOGRAPHY OF THE CENTURY

Foreword by

JOE NAMATH

DK PUBLISHING
www.dk.com

IN ASSOCIATION WITH THE NATIONAL FOOTBALL LEAGUE

NFL Properties Publishing Group

BEST SHOTS
THE GREATEST NFL PHOTOGRAPHY OF THE CENTURY

A DK PUBLISHING BOOK

Published in the United States by

DK Publishing, Inc.
375 Hudson Street
New York, New York 10014

10 9 8 7 6 5 4

Copyright © 1999, 2002 DK Publishing, Inc. and NFL Properties LLC.

Library of Congress Cataloging-in-Publication Data

Best shots : the greatest NFL photography of the century. --
    1st American ed.
        p.   cm.
    "In association with the National Football League."
    ISBN 0-7894-8075-1 (alk. paper)
    1. National Football League Pictorial works. I. DK Publishing.
Inc. II. National Football League. III. Title: Greatest NFL
photography of the century.
GV955.5.N35B47 1999
796.332'64'0973--dc21   99-23273
                                                  CIP

Produced by NFL Creative.
6701 Center Drive West, Suite 1111
Los Angeles, California 90045

Editor-in-Chief: John Wiebusch
General Manager: Bill Barron
Managing Editor: Chuck Garrity, Sr.
Best Shots Editor: Tom Barnidge
Best Shots Executive Art Director: Brad Jansen
Associate Art Director: Evelyn Javier
Director-Photo Services: Paul Spinelli
Photo Editor: Kevin Terrell
Manager-Photo Services: Tina Resnick
Director-Manufacturing: Dick Falk
Director-Print Services: Tina Dahl
Publishing Manager: Lori Quenneville
DK Editor: Alrica Green

Printed in Hong Kong by South Seas.

DK Publishing books are available at special discounts for bulk purchases for sales promotions or premiums. Special editions, including personalized covers, excerpts of existing guides, and corporate imprints can be created in large quantities for specific needs. For more information, contact Special Markets Dept./DK Publishing, Inc./ 375 Hudson Street/New York, New York 10014/Fax: 212-689-5254

BEAR ON THE LOOSE
(PAGE 1)
NO HURDLE WAS TOO HIGH FOR WALTER
PAYTON OF THE CHICAGO BEARS.
PHOTOGRAPH BY AL MESSERSCHMIDT, 1979.

VICTORY LAP
(PAGES 2-3)
LESTER HAYES OF THE RAIDERS
HAD THE WORLD AT HIS FEET.
PHOTOGRAPH BY JIM CHAFFIN, 1984.

because the collisions you experience in football are contrary to good health.

In a similar vein, I like the picture of Mike Curtis trying to rip off Roman Gabriel's head on page 12—and let's face it, that's exactly what the Mad Dog is trying to do. I'm just glad it wasn't me because Roman sure got caught in an awkward position. You see a lot of head-hunting shots in the old black-and-white pictures. You don't see those kinds of shots today because head-hunting is illegal now.

Sometimes when we think back to the football players of yesteryear and compare them to the players today, we have a tendency to say, "The modern athletes are so much better." But when I look at those old-timers running, and throwing, and tackling—even though they are still photos, you see the athleticism there. If you don't believe me, flip to page 44.

Then there's the spread on pages 138 and 139—a couple of old quarterbacks from Pennsylvania. I can relate to Joe Montana on the right. He's in the calm before the storm, that feeling of getting ready. You've collected yourself, and even though you feel quick as a cat you just try and let it stay cool and calm. Then I look at myself on the sideline in that other picture, and it doesn't bring back any good memories at all because I know something's wrong. A broken wrist or a shoulder injury, I believe.

You like the fur coat? Me, too! It's fun seeing all the details of that scene now.

I see Larry Csonka on page 73, and right away I notice Larry's ball hand. When I look at this picture I see that big old claw of his squeezing that ball, and I can understand why he was so good at not fumbling over the years. Now turn to page 158. The mud is fun, but I like the picture because it shows there's more than one battle going on during every play. It's a team game, but three individual battles are raging.

It's the little things, the details, that I enjoy most. Take page 126, for instance. That's a nice convoy Jim Taylor has picked up, but I'm looking at Bart Starr. Sure enough, he's checking out that back side of the defense after handing off, making sure no defenders are trailing the play.

That photo of the Packers' sweep makes me think of Super Bowls I and II, and where I was when Vince Lombardi's teams played those games. And that's what a lot of these pictures do for all of us. They generate memories of where we were or what we were doing at a certain time.

It isn't just football photos that have such power. When I see the famous picture of Muhammad Ali standing over Sonny Liston, I know exactly where I was. I had to listen to the fight on the radio. But when I saw the picture, it brought back such a stream of memories. Not just of that fight, but of where I was in my life at that time. Secretariat in the Belmont, coming down the home stretch with no other horse in sight—it's the same thing.

There's a picture I've seen a dozen times of myself running out for introductions before a game at Shea Stadium. The stands are packed, and we're ready for work. Even today, it brings back strong feelings. When I see that picture, I just get goose bumps.

Turn through the pages of this book and you might get a few of your own. ▮

BROADWAY JOE
JOE NAMATH ALLOWED HIMSELF A LITTLE SMILE AFTER
THE JETS UPSET THE COLTS IN SUPER BOWL III.
PHOTOGRAPH BY DARRYL NORENBERG, 1969.

STAYING FOCUSED

BY TOM BARNIDGE

Photographers will tell you that covering a pro football game is like no other assignment in sports. The opportunities for great images are limitless—and so are the challenges that the game poses.

The weather can be scorching...or freezing...or wet. The sun can disappear behind a cloud one instant...and return the next. The ball carrier can break out of focus in a flash, or he can come flying directly into your lap. A forward pass can become an interception, which results in a fumble that is run back in the other direction. All the while, the photographer must maneuver for shooting position while reaching for the camera with the correct lens.

"Nothing is predictable and everything is changing," photographer Al Messerschmidt says, "but my success depends on being consistent—consistent in getting the best possible pictures."

Messerschmidt succeeds far more often than he fails, as evidenced by the photograph that appears on page 1 of this book. His classic photograph of Walter Payton, hurdling Tampa Bay defenders while searching the field for more running room, is the defining image of the NFL's all-time leading rusher.

Messerschmidt is only one of the dozens of outstanding photographers whose work is showcased in *Best Shots*, where victory and defeat are captured on film, and energy and mood are frozen in time.

Peter Read Miller's ominous portrait of Oakland Raiders quarterback Ken Stabler as he approached the line of scrimmage in 1977 (page 77) evokes the unmistakable image of a gunslinger

in the Old West who is aching for a fight.

"Back in those days, the Raiders sauntered onto the field with a cocky, top-gun attitude," Miller says, "and that picture seemed to sum it up."

A sharp contrast can be found on page 139, where Michael Zagaris captured quarterback Joe Montana leaning against a wall alone with his thoughts in the final minutes before the kickoff of Super Bowl XXIII.

"I've always liked to take people behind the scenes," Zagaris says, "to take people to places they never have been. I want them to feel what it's like to be a player in those situations."

Tony Tomsic, with an eye for the allure of pro football's power and grit, has snapped many memorable scenes, but few better than the photo of Green Bay coach Vince Lombardi (page 48), still exulting in victory more than three decades after his Packers defeated the Dallas Cowboys to win the 1966 NFL title.

"Tony is the midwestern, black-and-blue, old-school football sort of guy," Miller says. "He's been around for a while. He started as a newspaper photographer, and he was among the first to see the game as something special."

The images that make *Best Shots* come alive are the same scenes that propelled the National Football League to unparalleled popularity.

The 49ers' Jerry Rice is caught in midflight, magically clutching a fingertip catch...Jim Taylor grits his teeth and accelerates behind his blockers in the fabled Green Bay power sweep...the Vikings' Alan Page emerges from a pile of bodies to thrust his hand upward to block a field-goal attempt. The images are old and new, black-and-white and color, spanning the game's past and its present.

In the end, there is but one common thread that brings all of the pages in *Best Shots* together: the unique skills of the gifted photographers who have chronicled pro football.

What are the elements that define the great ones?

"A lot of things go into it," Messerschmidt says. "Part of it is knowledge of the sport. Part of it is being in the right place at the right time. Part of it is being knowledgeable about film, equipment, and lighting. And part of it is luck. Just plain luck. If you're at one end of the field when a touchdown is scored at the other end, there's not much you can do about it."

Field position is as much a part of pro football photography as it is a part of the game.

"The fact is, there is no one perfect spot to set up," Miller explains. "You have to make choices based on your feelings about the game, and you can be right or wrong.

"In a lot of other sports, you are more restricted. In basketball, you shoot under the basket. In baseball, you shoot from assigned photo positions. But in football, you can go in this end zone or that one, this sideline or the other. That's what makes it the most fun and the most challenging. You have a direct input in how successful your shoot will be."

But the best photographers, everyone concedes, do more than snap their shutters at game action. They see subtleties that capture the atmosphere that surrounds each game. The mud-caked face of a weary lineman....the anguished expression of a beaten foe...the single-minded focus of a coach seeking answers from a clipboard.

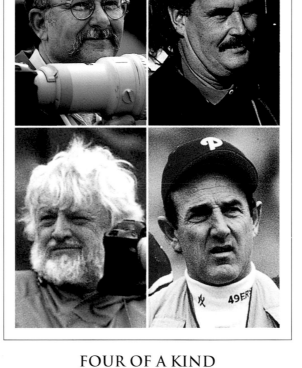

FOUR OF A KIND

AMONG THE BEST PHOTOGRAPHERS IN THE BUSINESS
(CLOCKWISE FROM TOP LEFT): AL MESSERSCHMIDT,
PETER READ MILLER, MICHAEL ZAGARIS, AND TONY TOMSIC

"Your imagination is the key," Messerschmidt says. "You can sit on the sidelines and shoot running backs all day. But in my opinion, some of the most memorable shots are the photographs with an entirely different feel."

"I especially like the mood stuff," Zagaris says. "It's not that I don't like action. But the mood shots can be special."

In 1980, Miller focused tightly on cornerback Lester Hayes's hands (page 136), which were layered with an extra-heavy application of "stickum," a gel-like substance designed to make catching passes easier. Suddenly, the defensive back's numerous interceptions were easier to understand.

Messerschmidt let his artistic inclinations take over when he attended the Dallas Cowboys' training camp in 1993 (page 148). Beyond the open end of the stadium in Austin, Texas, where the team was working out, he noticed that the early-evening sun was about to disappear on the horizon.

"I borrowed a stepladder from a TV guy so I could get up high and shoot straight into the sun," he says, "and I positioned myself in line with the players' silhouettes. I had about three minutes to get the shot because from the time the sun goes orange until it sets, things change in a hurry."

But the photographers whose work appears in *Best Shots* rarely have been caught unprepared. Capturing NFL moments has become their passion. The hardest part for any of them is determining which ones they like best.

"That's difficult," Zagaris says. "It's like asking a parent who has seven children which one is his favorite. You love all of your children differently but equally." ◼

MAIN MAN

JOHN ELWAY RECEIVED A WARM WELCOME ON A COLD DAY WHEN HE JOINED
HIS DENVER BRONCOS TEAMMATES IN PREGAME INTRODUCTIONS.
PHOTOGRAPH BY JOHN BETANCOURT, 1987.

▲ CRUNCH TIME
LINEBACKER MIKE CURTIS OF THE COLTS PUT AN
ABRUPT END TO THE FORWARD PROGRESS OF
RAMS QUARTERBACK ROMAN GABRIEL.
PHOTOGRAPH BY MALCOM EMMONS, CIRCA 1968.

HERO'S WELCOME ▶
QUARTERBACK RANDALL CUNNINGHAM, THEN A
STAR WITH THE EAGLES, BASKED IN THE GLOW
OF ADMIRING PHILADELPHIA FANS.
PHOTOGRAPH BY MICHAEL MERCANTI, 1990.

A JOB WELL DONE

Even an opposing fan expressed his appreciation to Lions quarterback Erik Kramer at the end of a hard day's work. Photograph by Joe DeVera, 1992.

◄ **HATS OFF**

CHARGERS RUNNING BACK KENNY BYNUM WAS
HAPPY JUST TO HOLD ON TO THE FOOTBALL WHEN
THE CHIEFS' REGGIE TONGUE CAME CALLING.
PHOTOGRAPH BY THEARON HENDERSON, 1998.

FALLING STARS ▲

RODNEY HAMPTON WAS ON THE BOTTOM LOOKING UP
WHEN THE DALLAS COWBOYS' DEFENSE ARRIVED AT
ONCE AND SMOTHERED THE RUNNING BACK.
PHOTOGRAPH BY SETH HARRISON, 1994.

JAGUAR ON T[...]
Mammoth tackle Tony Bosel[...]
no secret of his annoyance[...]
the Browns and a relu[...]
Photograph by Rich[...]

THE SHIRT OFF HIS BACK
CARDINALS WIDE RECEIVER MEL GRAY WAS WILLING
TO MAKE ANY SACRIFICE TO ESCAPE THE GRASP OF
NEW YORK GIANTS DEFENDERS.
PHOTOGRAPH BY BOB HOLT III, 1978.

25

CONCENTRATION
WEBSTER SLAUGHTER KEPT HIS EYES
ON THE PRIZE AS HE EXTENDED HIMSELF
FOR A FINGERTIP RECEPTION.
PHOTOGRAPH BY MARK A. DUNCAN, 1991.

BETWEEN BATTLES

GREEN BAY DEFENDERS, MUDDIED AND WEARIED, CAUGHT
A BREATHER ON THE SIDELINE WHILE THEIR TEAMMATES
ON OFFENSE WENT TO WORK.
NATIONAL FOOTBALL LEAGUE PHOTOGRAPH, CIRCA 1963.

JUMPING JACK

QUARTERBACK JACK KEMP OF THE BUFFALO BILLS LITERALLY TOOK
TO THE AIR IN A GAME AGAINST THE HOUSTON OILERS.
PHOTOGRAPH BY LOU WITT, 1963.

HEAD-HUNTER

BEN DAVIDSON OF THE OAKLAND RAIDERS, WHO PACKED
275 POUNDS ON A 6-FOOT 8-INCH FRAME, MADE SHORT
WORK OF MIAMI QUARTERBACK BOB GRIESE.
PHOTOGRAPH BY RON RIESTERER, 1970.

BLOCK PARTY

The long arm of Alan Page was unmistakable as
the Minnesota Vikings blocked a field-goal
attempt by the Chicago Bears.
Photograph by Fred Anderson, 1977.

ARTIST AT WORK

JERRY RICE, THE LEADING RECEIVER IN THE HISTORY OF
THE NFL, DEMONSTRATED THE GRACEFUL FORM THAT
ELEVATED HIM TO A CLASS OF HIS OWN.
PHOTOGRAPH BY BILL FOX, 1987.

EUPHORIA

WIDE RECEIVER IRVING FRYAR MADE NO SECRET OF HIS
FEELINGS AFTER SCORING FOR THE MIAMI DOLPHINS.
PHOTOGRAPH BY GLENN OSMUNDSON, 1994.

LION IN FLIGHT
Running back Billy Sims of the Detroit Lions ran
with a grace that seemed to defy gravity.
Photograph by Peter Read Miller, 1980.

WEATHER OR NOT
Neither LeRoy Butler of the Packers nor a driving
rain could keep Baltimore's Derrick Alexander
from making a wet reception.
Photograph by John McDonnell, 1996.

AERIAL ACT

Wide receiver John Jefferson fully extended himself to make a fingertip reception for the San Diego Chargers. Photograph by Michael Yada, 1980.

FALL GUYS

Green Bay safety Darren Sharper had his hands full when he tackled Panthers running back Anthony Johnson. Photograph by Bernie Nuñez, 1998.

DETERMINATION
DERRICK FENNER (34) OF THE RAIDERS HAD ONLY ONE DESTINATION
IN MIND WHEN HE COLLIDED WITH THE WASHINGTON REDSKINS.
PHOTOGRAPH BY ROBERT A. MARTIN, 1995.

SIGNS OF THE TIMES
The New York Giants and Brooklyn Dodgers squared off at
the Polo Grounds before a backdrop of sponsor messages.
Photograph by Wide World Photos, 1936.

▲ JUMPING FOR JOY

After scoring a touchdown, the Giants' Mark
Ingram celebrated in the end zone.
Photograph by Jim Cooper, 1991.

TUG OF WAR ▶

Kenneth Davis (23) of the Bills met his match when
he tried to get past the Cowboys' Ken Norton, Jr.
Photograph by Eric Risberg, 1992.

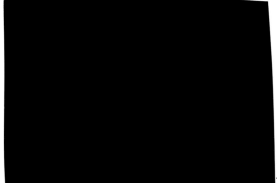

A GAME TO REMEMBER ▲
KELLEN WINSLOW (80), EXHAUSTED AFTER STARRING
IN AN OVERTIME PLAYOFF VICTORY, HAD TO BE
HELPED OFF THE FIELD BY CHARGERS TEAMMATES.
PHOTOGRAPH BY AL MESSERSCHMIDT, 1981.

SACK TIME ▲
QUARTERBACK STEVE YOUNG OF THE 49ERS RECEIVED A SURPRISE
VISIT FROM FALCONS' LINEBACKER JESSIE TUGGLE.
PHOTOGRAPH BY KEVIN TERRELL/NFLP, 1998.

◄ SPLASHDOWN
TAMPA BAY'S RICKY BELL PREPARED FOR A WET LANDING AFTER
COLLIDING WITH ART STILL OF KANSAS CITY.
PHOTOGRAPH BY ERIC MENCHER, 1979.

SNOW FUN

A BLIZZARD OBLITERATED YARD LINES AND OBSCURED VISION,
BUT THAT DIDN'T STOP THE PHILADELPHIA EAGLES FROM
WINNING THE 1948 NFL CHAMPIONSHIP GAME.
NATIONAL FOOTBALL LEAGUE PHOTOGRAPH, 1948.

A DIRTY JOB
THE DOLPHINS' A.J. DUHE, BOB BAUMHOWER, AND DOUG
BETTERS BATTLED THE ELEMENTS AND WON.
PHOTOGRAPH BY AL MESSERSCHMIDT, 1983.

TOUCHDOWN!
Muhsin Muhammad flew into the end zone, football first, to score against the Green Bay Packers. Photograph by Bernie Nuñez, 1998.

◆ SO CLOSE, SO FAR

TRY AS THEY MIGHT, NEITHER WILLIE GREEN (86) OF
THE PANTHERS NOR THE PACKERS' TYRONE WILLIAMS
COULD CATCH UP WITH A TANTALIZING PASS.
PHOTOGRAPH BY BENNY SIEU, 1996.

SUCCESSFUL LAUNCH ▶

DESPITE THE LONG ARMS OF THE BALTIMORE COLTS'
DEFENDERS, THE CLEVELAND BROWNS CONVERTED
AN EXTRA-POINT ATTEMPT.
PHOTOGRAPH BY TONY TOMSIC, 1971.

ROUGH LANDING

Anthony Miller of the Chargers landed with a thud...
and without the ball, when Cincinnati's
David Fulcher helped him to the ground.
Photograph by Robert Gauthier, 1991.

◀ **A GAME OF EMOTION**

CAROLINA PANTHERS LINEBACKER LAMAR LATHON DIDN'T
HESITATE TO EXPRESS HIS FEELINGS FROM THE SIDELINE
TO HIS TEAMMATES ON THE FIELD.
PHOTOGRAPH BY SCOTT CUNNINGHAM, 1995.

JUMP BALL ▲

THE PITTSBURGH STEELERS AND LOS ANGELES RAMS
MUSCLED FOR POSITION AS A PRIZE TUMBLED
GENTLY FROM THE SKY.
PHOTOGRAPH BY LONG PHOTOGRAPHY, 1993.

◄ NOW YOU SEE HIM...

ALMOST FROM THE MOMENT HE ARRIVED IN
THE NFL, BARRY SANDERS'S TRADEMARK WAS
HIS UNCANNY ABILITY TO CHANGE DIRECTIONS.
PHOTOGRAPH BY ALLEN KEE, 1995.

PAPA BEAR ▲

BEARS FOUNDER AND COACH GEORGE HALAS
BEAMED WITH PRIDE AFTER HIS TEAM CRUSHED
WASHINGTON 73-0 IN THE NFL TITLE GAME.
PHOTOGRAPH BY UPI, 1940.

▲ THE FACE OF VICTORY

Hard-working tackle Forrest Gregg, a member of
the Pro Football Hall of Fame, was an integral
part of the Packers' success in the 1960s.
Photograph by Robert Riger, circa 1963.

◀ NEAR MISS

EAGLES CORNERBACK MARK MCMILLIAN (29) AND RAMS
WIDE RECEIVER ISAAC BRUCE COULD ONLY WAVE AT A
SPIRALING PASS THAT ESCAPED THEIR GRASPS.
PHOTOGRAPH BY GEORGE REYNOLDS, 1995.

DIFFERENCE OF OPINION ▲

QUARTERBACK STEVE YOUNG OF THE 49ERS DIDN'T
ATTEMPT TO HIDE HIS FEELINGS WHEN HE TOOK
ISSUE WITH AN OFFICIAL RULING.
PHOTOGRAPH BY DINO VOURNAS, 1997.

▲ NIGHT LIGHT

A FULL MOON PEEKED IN ON THE ACTION AT
BUFFALO'S RICH STADIUM, WHERE THE BILLS AND
THE INDIANAPOLIS COLTS SQUARED OFF.
PHOTOGRAPH BY MIKE GROLL, 1992.

SOME PAIN, NO GAIN

A stampede OF Buffalo Bills defenders trampled Oakland Raiders quarterback Jay Schroeder. Photograph by Kevin Terrell/NFLP, 1991.

BREAKAWAY
Defensive tackle Joe Phillips tried in vain to slow the progress of Broncos running back Terrell Davis.
Photograph by Eric Lars Bakke, 1995

▲ SWANN DIVE

PITTSBURGH'S LYNN SWANN MADE A SPECTACULAR 53-
YARD CATCH IN SUPER BOWL X OVER THE OUTSTRETCHED
FORM OF DALLAS'S MARK WASHINGTON.
PHOTOGRAPH BY WARREN SKIPPER, 1976.

SURPRISE! ▶

QUARTERBACK TRENT DILFER OF THE BUCCANEERS
RECEIVED AN UNWANTED SURPRISE WHEN THE
VIKINGS' HENRY THOMAS ARRIVED FROM BEHIND.
PHOTOGRAPH BY STEVEN MURPHY, 1994.

◄ THE EYES HAVE IT

BEARS LINEBACKER MIKE SINGLETARY WAS THE PICTURE
OF CONCENTRATION WHEN HE SIZED UP QUARTERBACK
TIMM ROSENBACH OF THE CARDINALS.
PHOTOGRAPH BY PETER READ MILLER, 1990.

PORTRAIT OF A COWBOY ▲

THE UNMISTAKABLE SILHOUETTE OF LONG-TIME
COACH TOM LANDRY GRACED THE DALLAS COWBOYS'
SIDELINE FROM 1960-1988.
PHOTOGRAPH BY PAUL MOSELEY, 1988.

MARCHING INTO BATTLE

THE WASHINGTON REDSKINS HEADED ONTO THE FIELD BEFORE A
PRESEASON GAME WITH THE BUFFALO BILLS.
PHOTOGRAPH BY JOHN REID, 1983.

AUTUMN COLORS
A PAINTED SKY LOOKED DOWN ON BROWNS
FANS GATHERED AT CLEVELAND STADIUM.
PHOTOGRAPH BY GEORGE GOJKOVICH, 1986.

WHERE THERE'S A WILL...

WHEN A COLD DAY CHILLED THE BONES OF THE
CLEVELAND BROWNS' DEFENSIVE BACKS, THEY WARMED
THEMSELVES WITH A COAL FIRE IN A BUCKET NEAR THE BENCH.
PHOTOGRAPH BY TONY TOMSIC, 1958.

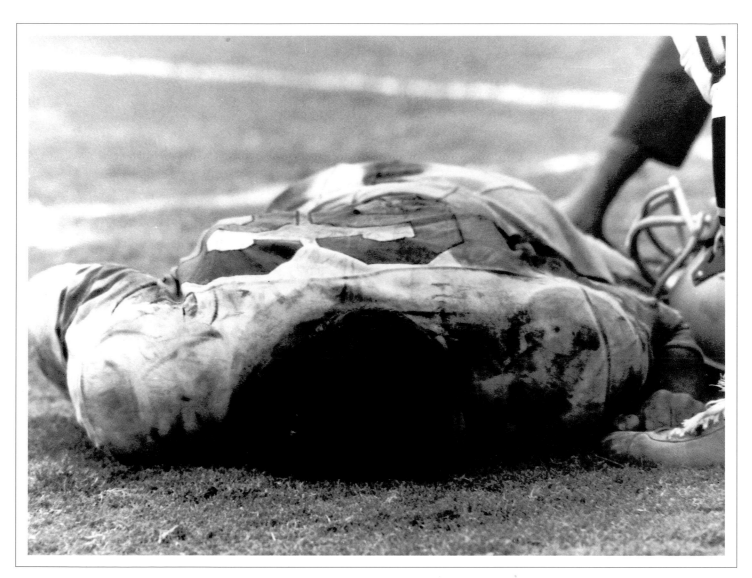

GROUNDED

THE PITTSBURGH STEELERS WERE BEATEN, AND GUARD
MIKE SANDUSKY WAS PHYSICALLY SPENT AFTER AN
EXHAUSTING DAY AGAINST THE LOS ANGELES RAMS.
PHOTOGRAPH BY DAVE BOSS, 1961.

CELEBRATION

Ronnie Lott of the 49ers had reason to smile after returning an interception 58 yards for a touchdown against Minnesota in an NFC playoff game. Photograph by Mickey Pfleger, 1990.

◀ TWIST AND REMOVE
SAFETY CARNELL LAKE TRIED TO REMOVE HAYWOOD
JEFFIRES'S HELMET AFTER THE HOUSTON
WIDE RECEIVER MADE A RECEPTION.
PHOTOGRAPH BY GAYLON WAMPLER, 1992.

CATCH AS CATCH CAN ▲
CHARLIE JOINER OF THE CHARGERS HAD SOME DIFFICULTY
HANGING ON TO THE FOOTBALL WHEN DENVER'S TONY
LILLY ARRIVED UNEXPECTEDLY.
PHOTOGRAPH BY ROB BROWN, 1985.

▲ SUPERSTAR
JIM BROWN WAS THE DOMINANT RUNNING BACK IN THE NFL FROM
1957-1965, WINNING EIGHT RUSHING TITLES IN NINE YEARS.
PHOTOGRAPH BY TONY TOMSIC, CIRCA 1961.

◄ WIDE OPEN SPACES
PERFECTLY EXECUTED BLOCKING ASSIGNMENTS BY HIS CHICAGO
BEARS TEAMMATES LEFT WALTER PAYTON WITH ROOM TO RUN.
PHOTOGRAPH BY FREDERIC STEIN, 1976.

SNOWBALL

The Minnesota Vikings tried to find
yardage while sorting their way
through the snow and the Packers.
Photograph by John Biever, 1977

SHOWTIME
BEARS WIDE RECEIVER DENNIS MCKINNON STRUTTED
HIS STUFF IN THE END ZONE FOR HOMETOWN FANS.
PHOTOGRAPH BY TONY TOMSIC, 1988.

COLLISION COURSE
RAIDERS CORNERBACK TERRY MCDANIEL (36) DIDN'T FIND MUCH
TO ENJOY ABOUT HIS MEETING WITH ERRIC PEGRAM.
PHOTOGRAPH BY DAN ROSENSTRAUCH, 1995.

▲ OUT OF THE WAY

UMPIRE NEIL GEREB HAD TO RUN FOR HIS LIFE WHEN
HE SUDDENLY SAW DAVID MEGGETT HEADED HIS WAY.
PHOTOGRAPH BY DAMIAN STROHMEYER, 1995.

BUCCANEER SANDWICH ▶

DEFENSIVE BACKS CHARLES MINCY AND ANTHONY PARKER
MADE CERTAIN THAT ANTONIO FREEMAN WENT NO FARTHER.
PHOTOGRAPH BY DAVID STLUKA, 1998.

◄ **ABOVE THE FRAY**
Oilers running back Earl Campbell found a
way to avoid the obstacles in his path.
Photograph by Pete J. Groh, 1979.

HAND-TO-HAND COMBAT ▲
The Saints' Jimmy Spencer and the 49ers'
Jerry Rice waged a battle for possession.
Photograph by Kevin Terrell/NFLP, 1995.

HEADY PLAY

The Rams' Eric Dickerson barely had begun to run when he ran headlong into Miami's Andy Hendel. Photograph by George Robarge, 1986.

▲ LEADER OF THE PACK

PACKERS COACH VINCE LOMBARDI INSPECTED HIS PLAYERS
AS THEY WERE INTRODUCED FOR THE NFL TITLE GAME.
PHOTOGRAPH BY VERNON BIEVER, 1967.

CHAMPIONSHIP SNEAK ▶

WHEN BART STARR (15) FOLLOWED JERRY KRAMER (64)
INTO THE END ZONE, THE PACKERS WERE NFL CHAMPIONS.
PHOTOGRAPH BY JOHN BIEVER, 1967.

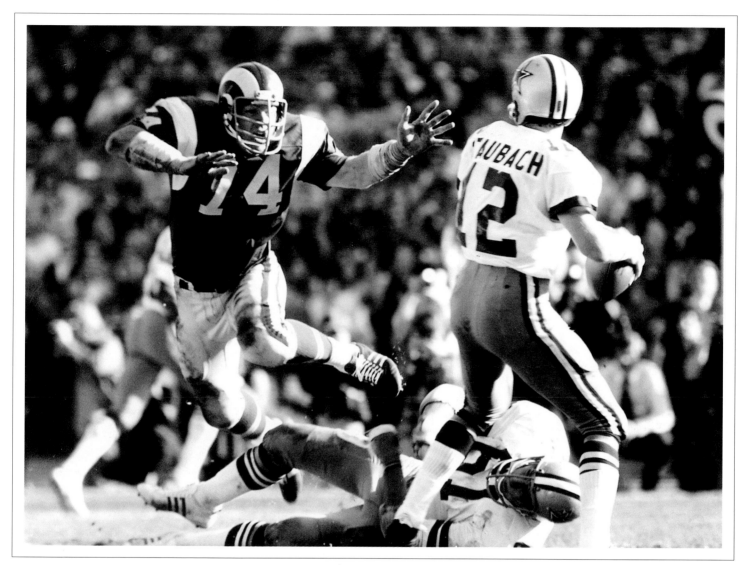

LONESOME COWBOY ▲

ROGER STAUBACH WAS ON HIS OWN WHEN THE RAMS'
MERLIN OLSEN ARRIVED IN THE DALLAS BACKFIELD.
PHOTOGRAPH BY JAMES E. FLORES, 1975.

▲ FOOTBALLET

PAUL COSTA (82) OF THE BILLS AND RON HALL (23) OF
THE PATRIOTS KEPT THEIR FOCUS ON THE FOOTBALL.
PHOTOGRAPH BY ROBERT L. SMITH, 1965.

BENCHED

Chicago Bears quarterback Jim McMahon found
time for a nap before a game against Tampa Bay.
Photograph by Al Messerschmidt, 1983.

◄ PERPETUAL MOTION

EVEN AS LINEBACKER RICHARD WOOD TRIED TO WRAP
HIM UP, WALTER PAYTON KEPT HIS LEGS CHURNING.
PHOTOGRAPH BY MARY STERLING/SARASOTA HERALD
TRIBUNE, 1979.

OPEN ARMS ▲

MOMENTS BEFORE HE MADE A RECEPTION, KANSAS
CITY WIDE RECEIVER STEPHONE PAIGE KEPT HIS EYES
FOCUSED ON THE BALL.
PHOTOGRAPH BY DAMIAN STROHMEYER, 1988.

PAYDIRT
RICK UPCHURCH WAS READY TO CELEBRATE AFTER
RETURNING A PUNT 78 YARDS FOR A TOUCHDOWN.
PHOTOGRAPH BY BARRY STAVER, 1982.

▲ TOO LITTLE, TOO LATE

SEATTLE DEFENDERS CONVERGED ON CLIFF BRANCH
SECONDS AFTER HE HAD MADE A NIFTY RECEPTION.
PHOTOGRAPH BY PETER READ MILLER, 1980.

UNWANTED VISITORS ▶

JIM NINOWSKI'S MUDDY PANTS WERE EVIDENCE OF A
LONG, HARD DAY AGAINST THE LOS ANGELES RAMS.
PHOTOGRAPH BY JAMES F. FLORES, CIRCA 1963.

RUN TO DAYLIGHT
ONE OF THE MOST FEARED SIGHTS IN THE NFL WAS THE GREEN BAY
PACKERS' POWER SWEEP THAT FEATURED JIM TAYLOR.
PHOTOGRAPH BY VERNON BIEVER, 1966

IN A FOG

When Drew Bledsoe's pass
emerged from a heavy fog, Terry
Glenn had beaten Rod Woodson
for a 53-yard gain.
Photograph by
Bernie Nuñez, 1997.

◀ **MOMENT OF TRUTH**

WIDE RECEIVER PATRICK JOHNSON OF THE RAVENS GAVE
HIS UNDIVIDED ATTENTION TO A PLUMMETING PASS.
PHOTOGRAPH BY DAVID STLUKA, 1998.

HEELS OVER HEAD ▶

UP BECAME DOWN FOR THE RAMS' BOB KLEIN WHEN HE
MET UP WITH FALCONS LINEBACKER TOMMY NOBIS.
PHOTOGRAPH BY DARRYL NORENBERG, CIRCA 1972.

GAME TIME

GLAD HANDS GREETED A MEMBER OF THE SAN DIEGO CHARGERS AS
HE WENT ONTO THE FIELD FOR PREGAME INTRODUCTIONS.
PHOTOGRAPH BY DIANE JOHNSON, 1998.

ALMOST
WIDE RECEIVER RON MORRIS OF THE CHICAGO BEARS
WATCHED HELPLESSLY AS THE BALL ESCAPED HIS GRASP.
PHOTOGRAPH BY DAVID DRAPKIN, 1991.

PURPLE PEOPLE EATERS
The famed defensive line of the Minnesota Vikings
presented a formidable obstacle for opposing kickers.
National Football League photograph, 1974.

GLUE FINGERS

THANKS TO THE LIBERAL USE OF "STICKUM," RAIDERS CORNERBACK
LESTER HAYES SELDOM DROPPED AN INTERCEPTION.
PHOTOGRAPH BY PETER READ MILLER, 1980.

FASHION PLATE

EVEN WHEN INJURY SIDELINED JETS QUARTERBACK JOE
NAMATH, HE WAS THE TEAM'S MOST STYLISH PLAYER.
PHOTOGRAPH BY VICTOR MIKUS, CIRCA 1973.

BEFORE THE BIG GAME

49ERS QUARTERBACK JOE MONTANA WAS ALONE WITH HIS
THOUGHTS IN THE MOMENTS BEFORE SUPER BOWL XXIII.
PHOTOGRAPH BY MICHAEL ZAGARIS, 1989.

FROZEN TUNDRA

Both Giants and Packers were chilled to the
bone in the 1962 NFL Championship game,
played in 13-degree temperature.
Photograph by Fred Roe, 1962.

▲ FOILED IN THE ACT

THE BILLS' JERRY BUTLER CAME AWAY EMPTY-HANDED,
THANKS TO THE TIGHT DEFENSE OF WILLIE BUCHANON.
PHOTOGRAPH BY ANDY HAYT, 1981.

CUT OFF AT THE PASS ▶

CORNERBACK DUANE STARKS OF THE RAVENS SOARED
ABOVE A PITTSBURGH RECEIVER FOR AN INTERCEPTION.
PHOTOGRAPH BY MARTY MORROW, 1998.

DOG DAYS OF SUMMER
A BROILING SUN BEAT DOWN ON THE DALLAS COWBOYS' TRAINING
CAMP IN AUSTIN, TEXAS.
PHOTOGRAPH BY AL MESSERSCHMIDT, 1993.

MUDDERS' DAY
Lem Barney (20) and Ken Sanders were faced with a dirty
job in bringing a Packers ball carrier to a stop.
Photograph by Vernon Biever, circa 1974.

◄ AIR DEFENSE

THE LONG ARM OF VESTEE JACKSON WAS ENOUGH TO FOIL
THE END-ZONE EFFORTS OF THE EAGLES' MIKE QUICK.
PHOTOGRAPH BY TONY TOMSIC, 1988.

HANDIWORK ▲

THE COWBOYS' MICHAEL IRVIN DISPLAYED RARE SKILLS IN
OUTDUELING CHAD SCOTT FOR A TOUCHDOWN RECEPTION.
PHOTOGRAPH BY TONY TOMSIC, 1997.

FLYING EAGLE

RANDALL CUNNINGHAM
TRAVELED BY AIR TO SCORE
AGAINST THE GIANTS.
PHOTOGRAPH BY GEORGE
REYNOLDS, 1989

ONE-POINT LANDING

Broderick Thomas of the Cowboys put an end to quarterback Steve Young's scrambling. Photograph by Paul Spinelli, 1996.

WIDE OPEN SPACES

Emmitt Smith looked hungrily downfield when he found himself running free. Photograph by Glenn James, 1996.

TURF WARS
BLOCKERS, DEFENDERS, AND BALL CARRIERS STRUGGLED
FOR FOOTING AS THE RAMS COLLIDED WITH THE VIKINGS
IN AN NFC DIVISIONAL PLAYOFF GAME.
PHOTOGRAPH BY PETER READ MILLER, 1977.

MY FRIEND, MY ENEMY
Steve Young and Brett Favre exchanged
sentiments after a hard-fought playoff game.
Photograph by Mickey Pfleger, 1997.